Royal Commission on the Distribution of Income and Wealth

an A to Z of Income and Wealth

Everyman's guide to the spread of income and wealth

London: Her Majesty's Stationery Office

Contents

Introduction   Page   3

INCOME

A   The spread of income   4
B   You and yours   5
C   Household incomes and needs   6
D   Lower income households   7
E   Thirty years of incomes   8
F   What goes in income tax?   9

WORK AND PAY

G   Earnings and other income   10
H   Pay — the narrowing gap   11
I   Age, sex and pay   12
J   Same job, different pay   13
K   Low pay   14
L   Benefits on top of pay   16
M   The changing workforce   17
N   The incomes of the self-employed   18
O   The self-employed: a closer look   19

WEALTH

P   What is wealth?   20
Q   How wealth is spread   21
R   The spread of wealth over the years   22
S   Bringing in pensions   23

KINDS OF WEALTH

T   Ingredients of wealth   24
U   How wealth is made up at different levels   25
V   Houses, company shares and land   26
W   Price effects   27

THE ACCUMULATION OF WEALTH

X   Savings and inequality   28
Y   The extent of inheritance   29

Z   A look abroad   29

Conclusion   29
Sources   30
Members of the Commission/   31
Previous Reports

Introduction

How does my income compare with others? How many very wealthy people are there in the UK — and how many very poor? How much do women get paid? What about fringe benefits? How about people who work on their own account? These and many similar topics are dealt with, and explained with the help of diagrams, in the pages that follow.

The best way to show how income and wealth are spread among the population is to divide the population into slices and find out how much each slice gets. If the top tenth of the population own five-tenths of the wealth, then those people have five times the national average. If the bottom 10% get only 2½% of the total income in the country, then they are getting a quarter of the average. In all this, however, we only discuss and compare elements of income and wealth that can be measured as amounts of money.

In a short report like this there is no room for technical details and qualifications, nor for lengthy discussion of definitions: there is, for example, more than one way of looking at income and many opinions about what should count as wealth. For full details reference should be made to the comprehensive studies provided in our other reports, listed on page 31. But we do look at the spread, or 'distribution', of income and wealth from as many angles as the figures — and the space — allow.

INCOME

A The spread of income

We start by adding up all the income received by everyone. The result for the 1976-77 tax year is £93 billion (ie £93,000,000,000). Earnings from employment and self-employment made up about four-fifths of this total and the rest was state pensions, other cash benefits and income from investment and property.

To show how this total is spread we 'line up' the 28½ million people who receive an income (married couples have been counted as one unit), placing those with the highest incomes at one end and those with the lowest at the other. We then divide this procession into ten equal parts and say how much each tenth takes of the total £93 billion.

The top bar shows how income before tax was spread in 1976-77. The second bar gives, for the same year, the distribution of income after tax (total after-tax income was £75 billion). How income tax affects individual people's incomes is shown later (in F); *the overall distribution is moved a step towards greater equality when income tax is taken into account.*

Population divided into tenths

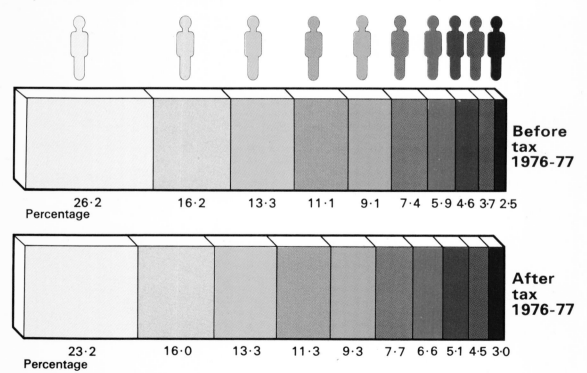

Before tax 1976-77

| 26·2 | 16·2 | 13·3 | 11·1 | 9·1 | 7·4 | 5·9 | 4·6 | 3·7 | 2·5 |

Percentage

After tax 1976-77

| 23·2 | 16·0 | 13·3 | 11·3 | 9·3 | 7·7 | 6·6 | 5·1 | 4·5 | 3·0 |

Percentage

B You and yours

Now we put in the money values.

When totting up your income to see where you come, remember that 'income' here includes everything you receive during the year — not only pay from your regular job but also cash benefits and any taxable income from other sources such as casual earnings, fees, profits and interest. Married people should add together the income of both partners. The figures shown in black are the incomes at the 'boundaries' between tenths in the 1976-77 distribution of income before tax. For example, if your income was between £3,282 and £3,972 you were in the fourth tenth, along with some 2,850,000 others.

Statistics for 1978-79 are not in yet, but approximate figures scaled up to mid-1979 are shown in red to give rough estimates of the boundaries at as recent a date as possible. *Where do you come?*

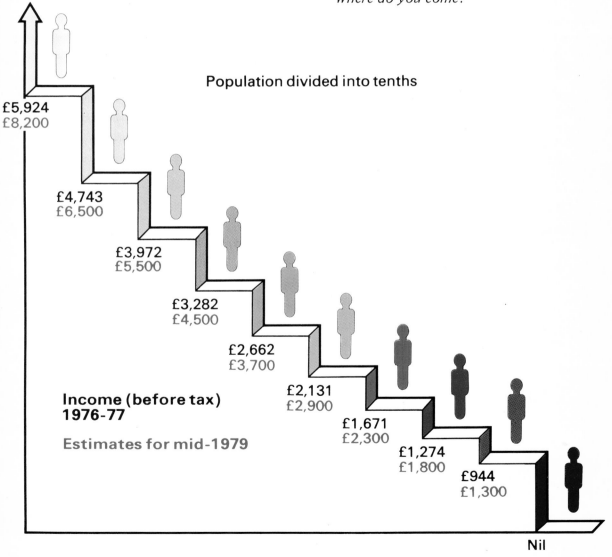

Population divided into tenths

£5,924
£8,200

£4,743
£6,500

£3,972
£5,500

£3,282
£4,500

£2,662
£3,700

Income (before tax) 1976-77

Estimates for mid-1979

£2,131
£2,900

£1,671
£2,300

£1,274
£1,800

£944
£1,300

Nil

C Household incomes and needs

A single man who lives alone may be just as well off as the man with a very much higher income who has to support a large family. So this bar shows what the distribution of income after tax looks like when some allowance is made for the differing needs of different households. The allowance is based on the Supplementary Benefit rates for different types of household as a rough indication of

relative needs. The effect of the adjustment is particularly noticeable at the lower end of the distribution where pensions and social security benefits — which vary with need — are so important.

Adjusted in this way, income is rather less unequally distributed; the top tenth of households has about five times as much income as the lowest tenth.

Population divided into tenths

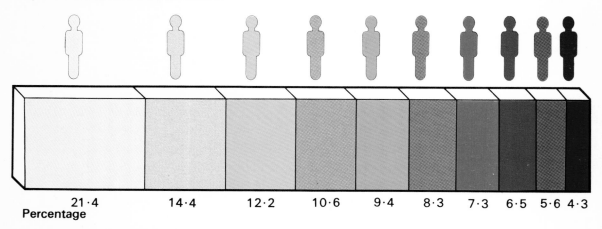

| 21·4 | 14·4 | 12·2 | 10·6 | 9·4 | 8·3 | 7·3 | 6·5 | 5·6 | 4·3 |

Percentage

Income after tax, adjusted to allow for differing needs of different households, 1976

D Lower income households

We now take a closer look at households on lower incomes, that is, those in the bottom quarter of the distribution of income adjusted to allow for differing needs. Employment is much less important as a source of income for the bottom quarter than for the population as a whole; indeed in over half of these households there is no-one earning at all. State pensions and social security payments are very important for people in these households, particularly for the elderly and for one-parent families.

The most numerous of the lower income recipients are the elderly and large families.

The diagram shows what proportions of different types of household fall in the bottom quarter. It indicates that *elderly people and one-parent families are the households most likely to be on lower incomes,* and — though this cannot be shown on the diagram — they do tend to stay there from year to year. A considerable proportion of other households who are on a lower income in one year will have moved out of the lower income category in the following year.

**1976
Percentage of
all households**

**Percentage on
lower incomes**

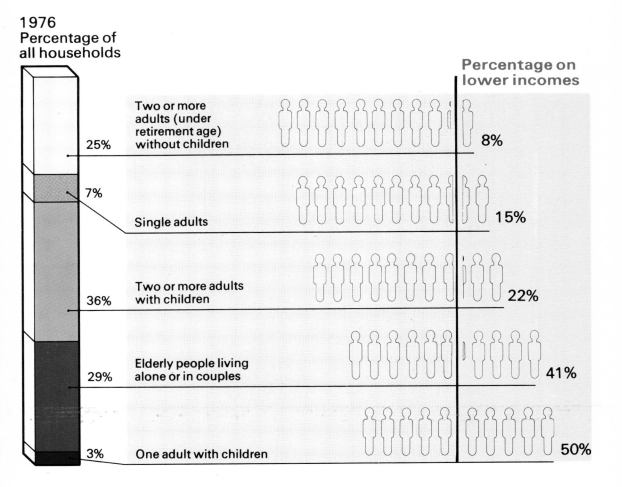

25%	Two or more adults (under retirement age) without children	8%
7%	Single adults	15%
36%	Two or more adults with children	22%
29%	Elderly people living alone or in couples	41%
3%	One adult with children	50%

E Thirty years of incomes

When looking at changes in the distribution of income over a long period, we have to go back to unadjusted figures as introduced on page A. As before, the figures cover income from all sources — earnings, pensions, cash benefits and income from investment and property.

Over the last thirty years successive falls in the share received by the top tenth have been largely retained in the top half of the spread. The top tenth gets less, the second, third, fourth and fifth tenths have come to get more. So *change has not been very pronounced except at the top; the share of the bottom half has not changed since 1949.*

Before tax

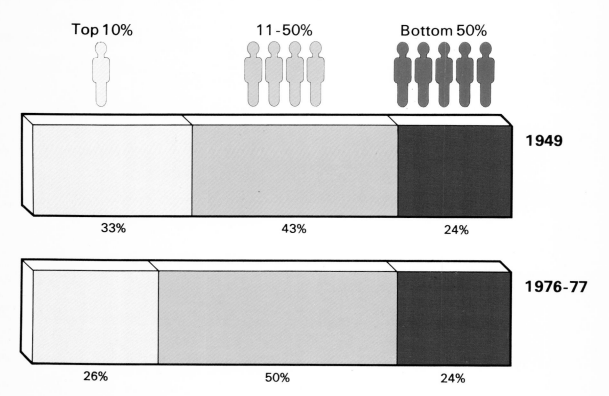

Top 10% 11-50% Bottom 50%

1949

33% 43% 24%

1976-77

26% 50% 24%

F What goes in income tax?

On average over 20% of income was paid in tax in 1976-77 against 10% in 1959. However much you earn, more of your income goes in tax than before: 20 years ago only the top tenth paid more than 10% of their incomes in tax, now the majority of the population do so.

Despite this change, people at the top still part with a much higher proportion of their incomes than those lower down.

Those at the top pay the most income tax, but everybody's tax has gone up.

Percentage of income paid in tax by different tenths of the population

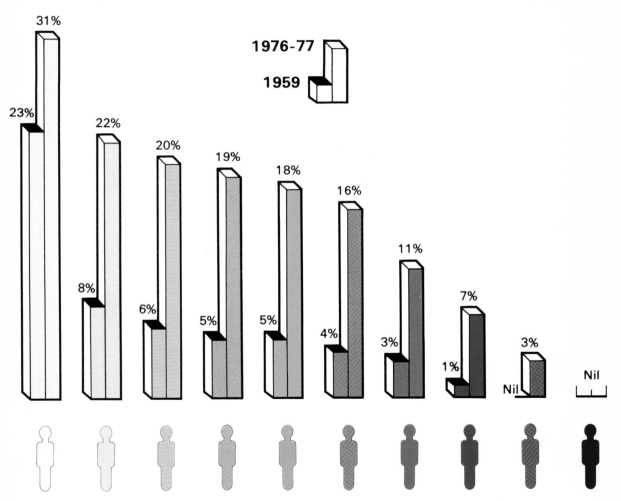

1976-77

1959

31%
23%
22%
8%
20%
6%
19%
5%
18%
5%
16%
4%
11%
3%
7%
1%
3%
Nil
Nil

G Earnings and other income

Before going on to look more closely at earnings, which are much the most important type of income for the population as a whole, we should note that the other types of income are far from negligible. Comparatively large proportions of the total income received by the top fifth, and even more by the top 1%, come from investment; and at the bottom, social security benefits are a major source of income. But *for the population as a whole earnings are most important.*

1976-77

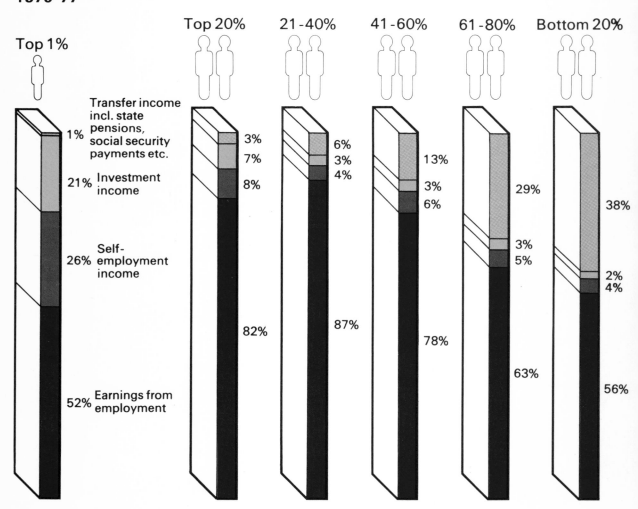

Top 1%

Top 20%

21-40%

41-60%

61-80%

Bottom 20%

Transfer income incl. state pensions, social security payments etc. — 1%

Investment income — 21%

Self-employment income — 26%

Earnings from employment — 52%

Top 20%: 3%, 7%, 8%, 82%

21-40%: 6%, 3%, 4%, 87%

41-60%: 13%, 3%, 6%, 78%

61-80%: 29%, 3%, 5%, 63%

Bottom 20%: 38%, 2%, 4%, 56%

H Pay-the narrowing gap

If you want to know whether someone earns more or less than you do, the first thing to find out is what kind of work he does. However, the differences between the average earnings of men in different occupations have become less in the course of this century, as the graph shows. Between 1913-14 and the 1950s the most striking change in pay structure was the narrowing of the higher professional workers' lead, but changes in recent years have been more general. Average earnings in different occupations have come to differ much less.

What kind of work you do makes less difference to your pay than it used to.

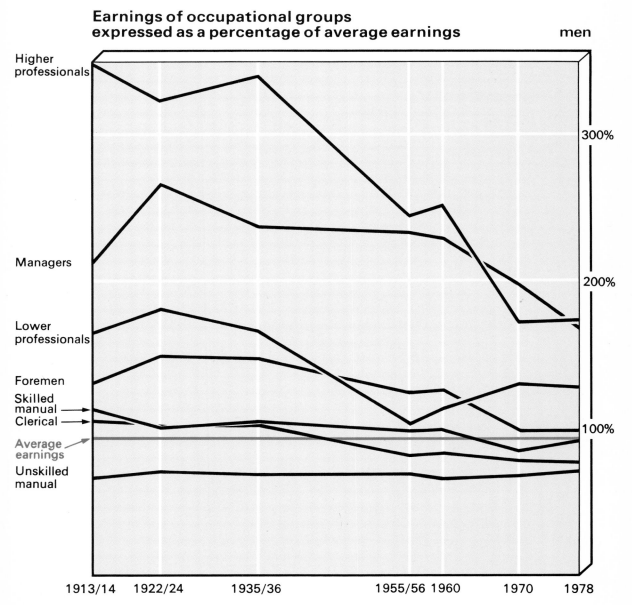

Earnings of occupational groups expressed as a percentage of average earnings   men

Higher professionals
Managers
Lower professionals
Foremen
Skilled manual →
Clerical →
Average earnings →
Unskilled manual

300%
200%
100%

1913/14   1922/24   1935/36   1955/56 1960   1970   1978

1. Age, sex and pay

Not only do we look at the way different jobs are differently paid, we have also tried to discover why people are paid more or less than others in the same broad occupational group. One factor is age, though how much pay is affected by age, and over what age ranges, depends very much on the type of work. Manual workers in their twenties get much more than teenagers, but their pay does not generally increase further as they get older; in their forties they usually start to earn less than younger men. On the other hand, a forty-year-old man in a non-manual job probably earns more than his colleagues ten and twenty years younger.

The graph also shows that, on average, women earn less than their male contemporaries. Usually when women and young people earn less than the average in a particular occupation it is because the jobs they are doing are the less well-paid ones.

Pay differs according to age and sex: by how much depends on the kind of work you do.

Average gross weekly earnings – full-time employment, April 1978

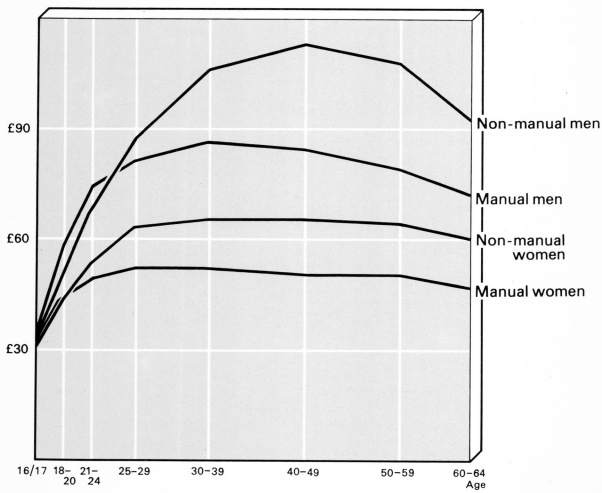

⅃ Same job, different pay

But even among adults of the same sex who are doing similar jobs we still find that actual earnings vary considerably. We have taken twelve very different occupations and for each one the variation is shown in the following way. We line up 100 adult men in that occupation in order of their earnings: the figures at the extremes are unreliable and so we leave out the top ten and the bottom ten and show the range of pay of the remaining eighty. So of 100 male mechanical engineers over 18 in April 1978, there were ten earning over £150 a week, and ten earning less than £77. The fiftieth man (the 'median') got £111.

Pay varies much more in some occupations than in others. Though on average farm

workers and cooks are both near the bottom of the scale, some cooks are relatively highly paid. Among farm workers pay does not vary so much. Notice also the way different jobs overlap. On the whole hospital doctors earn more than postmen, but there will be some postmen who are paid more than some doctors.

Earnings also vary a lot within individual industries. Indeed, knowing the industry someone works in generally tells you even less about his earnings than knowing his occupation. Age, seniority and overtime are other factors that may affect pay and so also is the size of the firm.

There is a wide range of earnings among people doing similar work.

Weekly earnings before tax (full-time men), April 1978

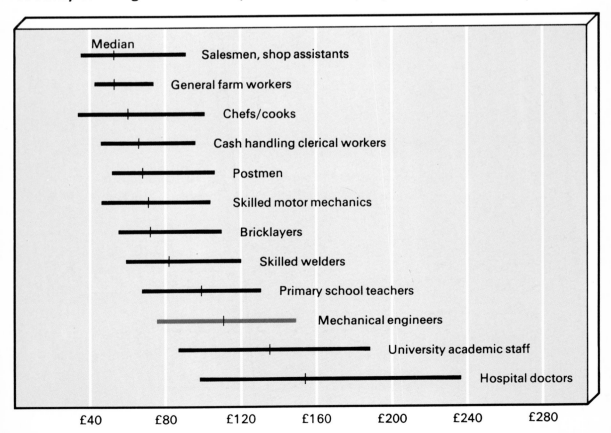

| Median | Salesmen, shop assistants |
| General farm workers |
| Chefs/cooks |
| Cash handling clerical workers |
| Postmen |
| Skilled motor mechanics |
| Bricklayers |
| Skilled welders |
| Primary school teachers |
| Mechanical engineers |
| University academic staff |
| Hospital doctors |

£40 £80 £120 £160 £200 £240 £280

K Low pay

There is no generally accepted definition of 'low pay'. We here describe someone as 'low paid' if he or she works full-time (this means 30 hours a week or more) and earns no more than those in the bottom tenth of male manual workers — a mid-1979 figure would be about £56 a week. If 10% of men doing full-time manual work are therefore counted as being low paid, then on the same basis so are 7% of men in non-manual jobs, 68% of women in manual jobs and 46% of women in non-manual jobs. All told, 72% of the low paid are women.

Low pay is not the same thing as a low standard of living: in fact less than one in five low paid workers belong to 'lower income' households (as defined in D). The low paid worker is often the household's second earner; indeed, it may be the wife's low paid job that saves the household from having to manage on a low income.

The chart shows that more of the manual workforce is low paid in some industries than in others, and for non-manual workers the picture is broadly similar though smaller proportions are low paid. Low pay is not confined to particular industries or occupations: for one thing, pay varies with age in all occupations, and even young professional people may earn low pay for a time. But *agriculture, the clothing and footwear industry and the distributive trades have particularly large proportions of low paid employees, and there is also a large contingent in public administration.*

1977

Percentage of manual workers on LOW PAY

All industries	10%	Men
	68%	Women
Agriculture	35%	
	Figures not available	
Clothing and footwear	25%	
	84%	
Construction	6%	
	Figures not available	
Transport and communication	4%	
	33%	
Distributive trades	27%	
	85%	
Public administration and defence	19%	Men
	54%	Women

1 Benefits on top of pay

So far we have considered only cash pay. This is considerably less than the total benefit to the employee from his employment, and also less than the total cost to the employer of employing him. The total cost includes, on top of pay, National Insurance and other payments the employer is legally bound to make, paid holidays and sick pay, and also benefits in kind, both those that are open to all employees and those limited to senior staff. The first four bars show that these benefits on top of pay are increasing in importance.

Many benefits in kind are open only to the most senior staff — who are also, in general, entitled to longer holidays than their juniors. The relative size of the benefits received by different grades of senior staff is shown by the five horizontal bars — these figures come from a different source and are not comparable with those illustrated in the other bars.

By and large, the more you earn, the larger percentage you get on top of pay.

Cost of benefits received as a percentage of wages and salaries

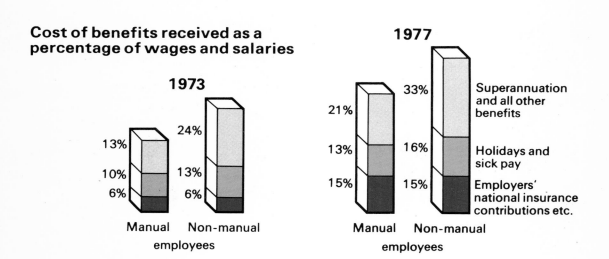

1973

Manual: 13%, 10%, 6%
Non-manual: 24%, 13%, 6%

Manual   Non-manual
employees

1977

Manual: 21%, 13%, 15%
Non-manual: 33%, 16%, 15%

Superannuation and all other benefits

Holidays and sick pay

Employers' national insurance contributions etc.

Manual   Non-manual
employees

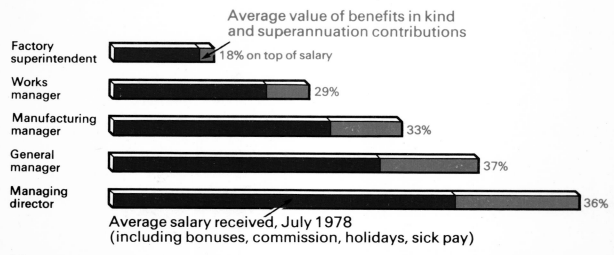

Average value of benefits in kind and superannuation contributions

Factory superintendent — 18% on top of salary

Works manager — 29%

Manufacturing manager — 33%

General manager — 37%

Managing director — 36%

Average salary received, July 1978
(including bonuses, commission, holidays, sick pay)

M The changing workforce

Between 1961 and 1978 men's average earnings increased in real terms (that is, in terms of what the money will buy) by about 40%, women's went up by more than 60%. At the same time, there was a tendency for people to move from lower to higher paid jobs.

These bars show how the workforce has changed since 1961.

In this period, for every 100 jobs, manual work has been supplanted by more highly paid work at the rate of nearly one job a year.

Men in the workforce

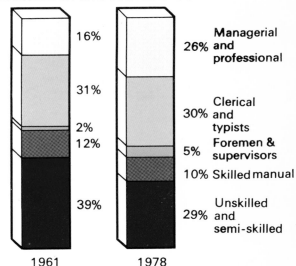

1961 — 18%, 7%, 5%, 36%, 34%

1978 — 32%, 5%, 8%, 32%, 23%

Women in the workforce

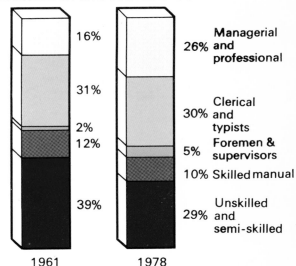

1961 — 16%, 31%, 2%, 12%, 39%

1978 — 26%, 30%, 5%, 10%, 29%

- 26% Managerial and professional
- 30% Clerical and typists
- 5% Foremen & supervisors
- 10% Skilled manual
- 29% Unskilled and semi-skilled

The biggest change in the composition of the workforce over the last 50 years has been the increase in the number of women, and more particularly of married women, who go out to work. This increase has maintained the size of the workforce as a percentage of the total population despite other changes that tended to make it smaller, such as the increase in the proportion of retired people.

There has been a big increase in the number of married women going out to work.

Total workforce

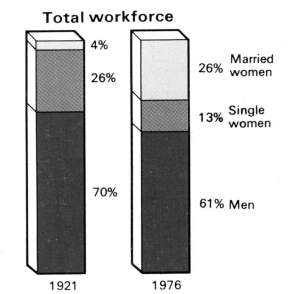

1921 — 4%, 26%, 70%

1976 — 26% Married women, 13% Single women, 61% Men

N The incomes of the self-employed

You are self-employed if you own and control the business you work for, whether it is a one-man firm or — at the other extreme — a limited company. Counting only people whose main source of income is from self-employment, there are altogether around two million self-employed, making up some 9% of the workforce. This is a smaller proportion than in other European countries and the proportion has been falling, both here and elsewhere in Europe.

The bar gives the spread of income (before tax) of the self-employed, dividing the total as usual between successive tenths of the self-employed population. It shows a much wider variation — for example, between the share of the top tenth and the share of the bottom tenth — than any of the other income distributions we have seen so far.

Self-employment is an area where under-recording of income presents particular difficulties. But the average recorded income of the self-employed is 70% higher than the average for employees. In making this comparison, it should be remembered that income from employment is reward for work, whereas self-employment income is a combination of reward for work and return on capital invested, having regard to the risk involved. Different kinds of self-employment require different levels of investment: most of a self-employed construction worker's income will be reward for work, but much more of a shopkeeper's income will be return on capital. This is one reason why the incomes of the self-employed differ more than those of the population as a whole.

The incomes of the self-employed are more widely spread than those of employees, and they are strongly represented at the top of the distribution.

Self-employed population divided into tenths

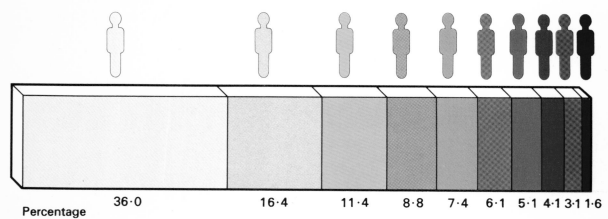

| 36·0 | 16·4 | 11·4 | 8·8 | 7·4 | 6·1 | 5·1 | 4·1 | 3·1 | 1·6 |

Percentage

Distribution of income before tax, 1974-75

○ The self-employed: a closer look

Closer inspection reveals that the wide spread of incomes can largely be explained by the very high incomes of a fairly small number of people, mainly those in the professions. One way of seeing this is to look at successive tenths of the distribution and find out the trades or professions of the people concerned. In the diagram we have done this, not for every tenth but for the top tenth, for the rest of the top half, and for the bottom half of the distribution.

The bars show clearly how the professional services are concentrated at the top. The main groups are lawyers, accountants, architects, engineers, doctors and dentists working on their own account. Although they are in all only 6% of the self-employed they constitute 35% of the top tenth. The other important self-employed trades — builders, farmers, and so on — are heavily represented in the middle and lower levels of the distribution.

The wide spread of incomes of the self-employed is due in part to the high incomes of the self-employed professionals.

Trade structure of different income groups, 1976-77

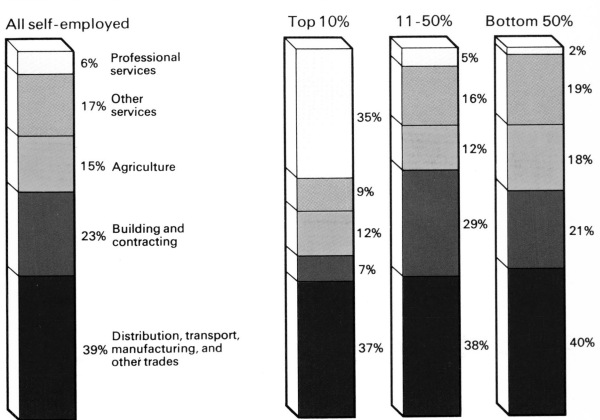

All self-employed
- 6% Professional services
- 17% Other services
- 15% Agriculture
- 23% Building and contracting
- 39% Distribution, transport, manufacturing, and other trades

Top 10%
- 35%
- 9%
- 12%
- 7%
- 37%

11-50%
- 5%
- 16%
- 12%
- 29%
- 38%

Bottom 50%
- 2%
- 19%
- 18%
- 21%
- 40%

P What is wealth?

Opinions differ about the kinds of possession (or 'asset') that should be counted as personal wealth. One possible definition is just those assets that can be bought and sold — 'marketable' assets, in other words. We adopt this definition in the next two pages.

Under a second possible definition all assets that do now or will in the future produce income are counted as wealth. This wider definition includes some types of asset which are very difficult to value — like 'human wealth', that is, the prospect of future earnings. Clearly we cannot present a distribution of wealth that goes all the way to satisfy this definition. What we can do is to add to marketable wealth one particular type of asset that cannot be bought or sold — pension rights. So in S, we look at the effect on the distribution of including rights to occupational and state pensions.

WEALTH

Q How wealth is spread

The information used in estimating the distribution of wealth comes from a variety of sources, and the estimates have to be built up in stages. All the same, this bar chart presents a reasonably reliable estimate of the distribution of wealth (that is, marketable wealth) among the adult population (18 and over).

Generally, the older people are, the more they are likely to own. Variation with age and the effect of inheritance together ensure that wealth is much less evenly spread than income. The top tenth of the population own a much bigger share of total wealth than the share of total income taken by the tenth with the highest incomes. So, when presenting the distribution of wealth, we need to subdivide the top tenth and show how much the top 1% owns, and the 2-5% and the 6-10% slices.

In 1976 the top 1% owned more marketable wealth than the whole of the bottom 80%.

Percentage of population owning wealth

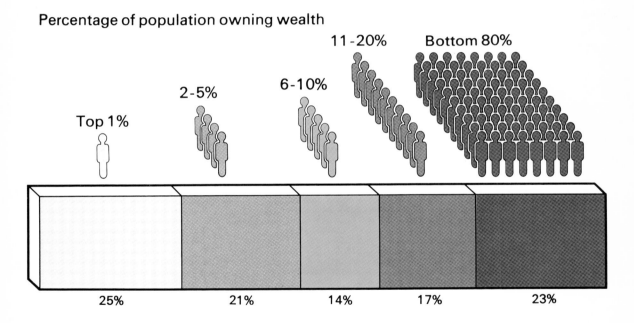

The distribution of wealth, 1976

R The spread of wealth over the years

During the last ten years the share of the top 1% has fallen appreciably, and the 2-5% slice has also come to hold less of total wealth. The other 95% of the population now own more — *the distribution has become less unequal.*

Though the figures are less reliable, estimates do go back as far as 1923. The top

1% then held about three-fifths of all the wealth, while the vast majority of the population, all those below the top 10%, owned about one-tenth. *Since the twenties the share of the top 1% has become much smaller.*

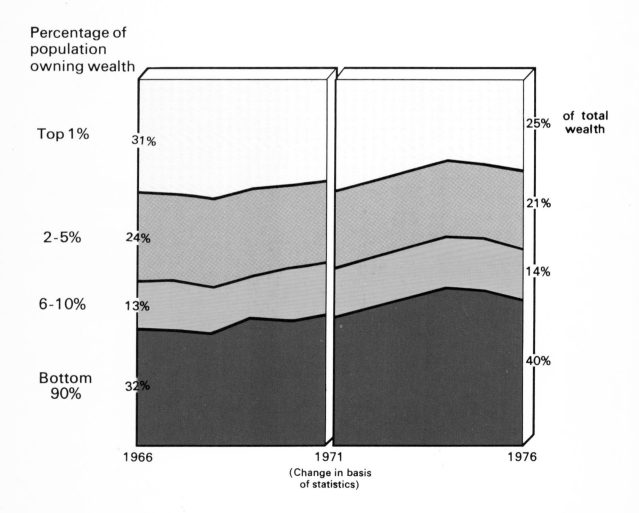

Percentage of population owning wealth

Top 1% — 31% ... 25% of total wealth

2-5% — 24% ... 21%

6-10% — 13% ... 14%

Bottom 90% — 32% ... 40%

1966   1971   1976

(Change in basis of statistics)

S Bringing in pensions

We now look at the effect on the distribution of including rights to pensions — while acknowledging that these rights, particularly to state pensions, differ in some important ways from marketable wealth. Approximate capitalised values can be worked out for both occupational and state pensions: on this basis the value of your pension increases steadily as you grow older, until you retire.

The first bar presents the basic distribution of wealth. Adding occupational pension rights into the distribution (middle bar) somewhat reduces the degree of inequality. The third bar shows that the addition of state pension rights has a marked levelling effect. *Including pension rights leads to a much less uneven distribution of wealth: with both occupational and state pensions included, the share of the bottom 80% is almost doubled.*

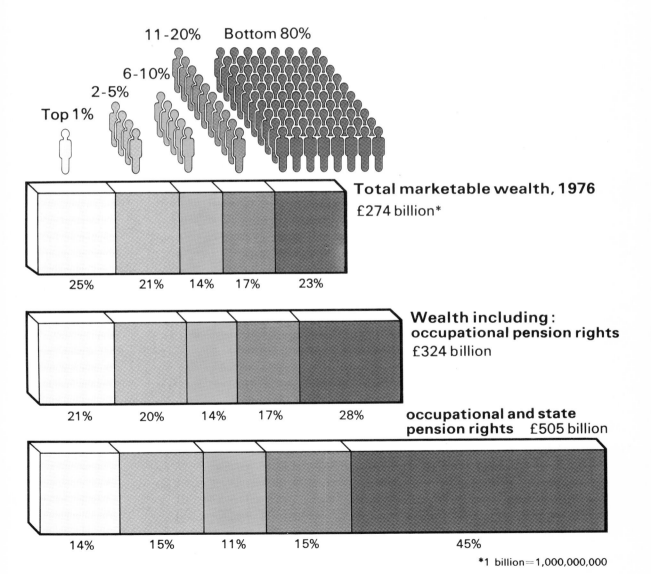

Total marketable wealth, 1976
£274 billion*

25%   21%   14%   17%   23%

Wealth including:
occupational pension rights
£324 billion

21%   20%   14%   17%   28%

occupational and state
pension rights   £505 billion

14%   15%   11%   15%   45%

*1 billion = 1,000,000,000

⊤ Ingredients of wealth

To calculate total personal wealth we add up the value of private individuals' holdings of all the main ingredients: houses, shares, savings in building societies, life assurance policies and so on, in fact, their holdings of all the various types of asset. These bars show how the different types of asset have varied in importance since 1960. For instance, in 1960, the homes people owned amounted to 19% of total personal wealth; in 1976 the proportion was 37% (though these figures make no allowance for mortgages and other debts).

The pattern of assets that people own has changed a lot since 1960.

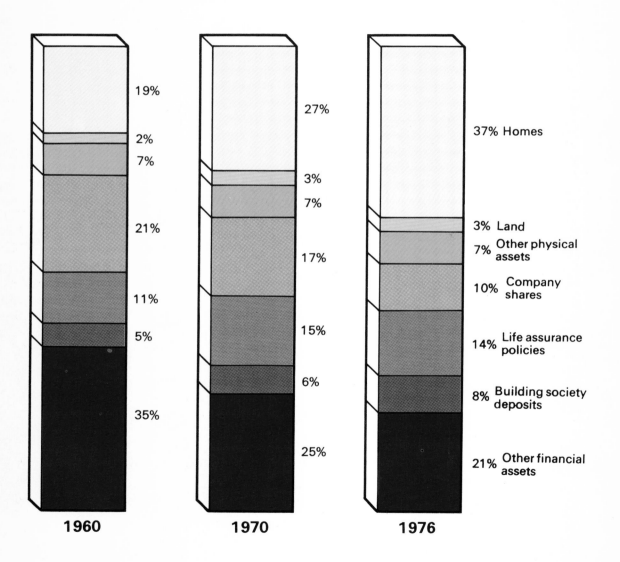

1960

19%
2%
7%
21%
11%
5%
35%

1970

27%
3%
7%
17%
15%
6%
25%

1976

37% Homes

3% Land

7% Other physical assets

10% Company shares

14% Life assurance policies

8% Building society deposits

21% Other financial assets

U How wealth is made up at different levels

The very wealthy do not just hold more of the assets held by the less well-off. The bars compare the amounts of each main ingredient that are found at three different levels of wealth: for the many who have less than £5,000, for those in the middle range between £10,000 and £20,000 and for the very wealthy over £200,000. *Shares and land are characteristic possessions of the very wealthy: for the less wealthy, homes and life assurance policies are more important.*

Total wealth holdings, 1976

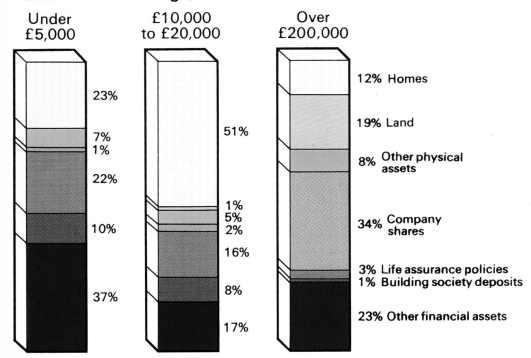

Under £5,000

£10,000 to £20,000

Over £200,000

23%
7%
1%
22%
10%
37%

51%
1%
5%
2%
16%
8%
17%

12% Homes
19% Land
8% Other physical assets
34% Company shares
3% Life assurance policies
1% Building society deposits
23% Other financial assets

Proportion of total holdings for which owners are in debt

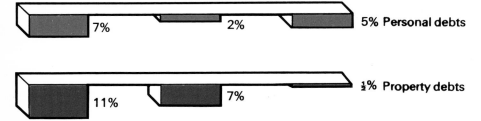

7%   2%   5% Personal debts

11%   7%   ½% Property debts

V Houses, company shares and land

There has been a steady increase in *home* ownership and at the same time houses have gone up in price more than other things. This has been to the advantage of people around the middle of the distribution and so has had an equalising effect on the spread of wealth.

Shares are a less popular form of wealth holding than they were twenty years ago: the proportion of 'listed' ordinary shares (those dealt with on the Stock Exchange) held by individuals has fallen from two-thirds to just over one-third, the balance having been taken up by pension funds, insurance companies, and other institutions. For all that, share ownership is very significant for the distribution of personal wealth because so much of it is concentrated at the top: as the diagram shows, the top 1 per cent owns more than half of all shares held by individuals.

The pattern of ownership for *land* (ie land other than that around houses) closely resembles that for shares.

The trend to home ownership has broadened the base of the wealth distribution.

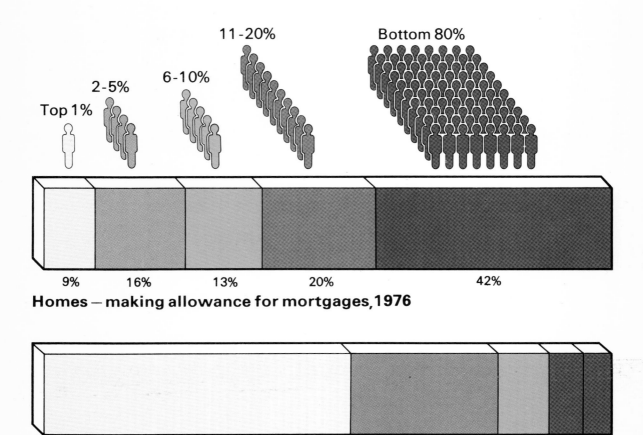

Homes – making allowance for mortgages, 1976

Top 1% 9% 2-5% 16% 6-10% 13% 11-20% 20% Bottom 80% 42%

Company shares, 1976

54% 26% 9% 6% 5%

W Price effects

The distribution of wealth can change because assets change hands, or because they change in value. If houses, for example, rise sharply in value then house-owners will have more wealth than before and those who hold their wealth in other forms will have (relatively) less.

The graph shows how the different assets have increased (or occasionally decreased) in price since 1960. For most of this period all the prices were increasing, though at different rates, and there was a genuine redistribution of assets underlying the change in the distribution. But in the last few years — since 1971 or 1972 — prices have been behaving differently, with house prices continuing to rise while share prices fell for a time. It is these price effects, rather than any change in what people actually possess, that have governed the trend in the distribution between 1972 and 1976. *Unsteady share prices and rising house prices have in recent years combined to show personal wealth as being spread more evenly.*

The 1960 price level for each asset = 100

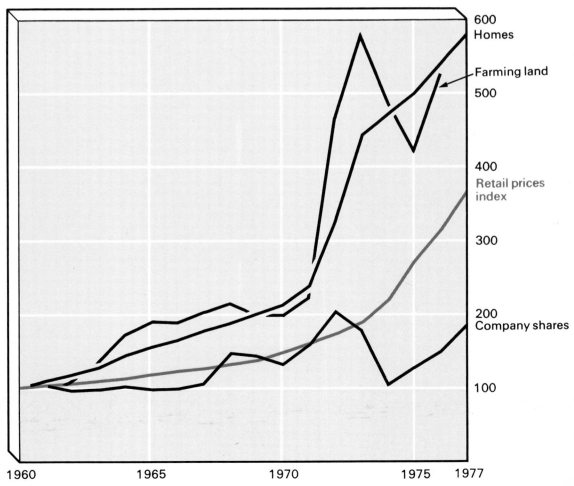

600
Homes

Farming land
500

400
Retail prices index

300

200
Company shares

100

1960   1965   1970   1975   1977

X Savings and inequality

Two ways of accumulating wealth can be investigated more closely. One way is by saving; the other is by receiving an inheritance or a gift. How much does each of these contribute to the inequality that we have found in the distribution of wealth?

One approach to the question is to estimate what the distribution would be if there were no inheritance, and the only way to accumulate wealth were to save as you earn. It would still be unequal, of course; people who earn more are able to save more and, at least up to retirement, the older you are the longer you will have had to accumulate savings.

We did a rough estimate, assuming a steady population and making assumptions about everything from the birth rate to the rate at which retired people use up their savings. Theoretical though this estimate is, setting it alongside the actual distribution of wealth suggests how much inequality can be generated purely and simply by the unequal distribution of savings.

Saving by itself makes for a distribution of wealth that is much more unequal than the distribution of income: but this still leaves a lot of inequality to be accounted for.

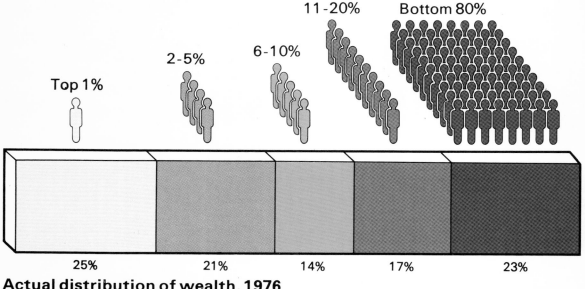

Actual distribution of wealth, 1976

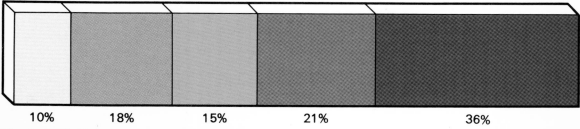

Notional distribution of savings

Y The extent of inheritance

If we start at the other end, and try to estimate how much of a person's wealth is the product of inheritance, we come up against an immediate difficulty. For instance, if you receive a legacy and either use it to start a business or invest it, so that it increases in value, should we count the capital gain as part of the legacy or as the result of your shrewdness as a businessman or investor?

What we can do, though, is to estimate the total value at current prices of existing wealth that was at one time or another 'transmitted' (that is, given or inherited) and to express this total as a fraction of total personal wealth. On this definition, *about a quarter of all wealth is transmitted.*

We know that the proportions are very different at different wealth levels and are much higher for the top 1% than lower down. We also know from surveys that, even though large holdings may be divided when their owners die, the wealth (at all levels) is largely retained by the late owner's relatives.

Z A look abroad

Because different countries investigate the distribution of income and wealth in different ways, straightforward comparison of the results is not possible. But there is enough information to give us a rough idea of how the UK compares with the other industrialised countries of the western world.

The distribution of income does not vary very much from one industrialised country to another, but on the whole it seems that the spread is more uneven in France, the USA, Japan, Canada and Germany than in the UK which, together with the Republic of Ireland, Sweden and Australia is towards the less uneven end of the scale.

Comparing *the distribution of wealth* is even more difficult. However the figures for Canada and the USA suggest that the top slices of the population in the UK own larger shares of total wealth than their counterparts in North America.

Conclusion

The Royal Commission has no axe to grind. Our job has been to present the facts — it is for others to draw conclusions. What we have done is to describe, in the most objective and accurate way possible, the many aspects of the spread of income and wealth in this country. The information given in this A to Z is offered in the hope that it will give a clearer understanding of the kind of society we live in.

Sources

	Diagrams	Text (where different)
A	Report No 7, Table 2.3	Economic Trends No 304, February 1979, page 88
B	Report No 7, Table 2.3; mid-1979 figures are Commission estimates (npe)	
C	Report No 6, Table 2.9	
D	Derived from Report No 6, Tables G.1, 2.10	Report No 6, Tables 2.11, 2.14, paragraph 5.121
E	Report No 7, Table 2.3	
F	Report No 7, Table 2.9 and supporting data (npe)	
G	Derived from Report No 7, Tables 2.14, 2.15	
H	Report No 8, paragraph 6.21 and Table 6.8	
I	Report No 8, Table 8.1	
J	Derived from Report No 8, Appendix H	
K	Report No 6, Tables M.20, M.21	Report No 6, Tables M.16, 2.14
L	Derived from Report No 8, Figure 9.2, and Report No 7, Table 2.22	
M	Derived from Report No 8, Tables 2.7, 2.6	Based on Report No 8, paragraph 6.11
N	Report No 8, Table 10.5	Report No 8, Table Q.1
O	Derived from Report No 8, Table 11.2	
Q	Report No 7, Table 4.4	
R	Report No 7, Table 4.4	Report No 7, Table 4.5
S	Report No 7, Figure 4.4	
T	Derived from Report No 5, Table 34 and Report No 7, Table 4.6	
U	Derived from Report No 7, Table 4.6	
V	Report No 7, Table 6.15	Report No 7, Table 6.4
W	Report No 7, Figure 5.1 and Table E.1	
X	Report No 7, Table 4.3 and Report No 5, Table K.2	
Y		Report No 5, paragraph 415
Z		Report No 5, Chapter 6; Report No 7, paragraphs 4.51-4.54

npe — not published elsewhere

ROYAL COMMISSION ON THE DISTRIBUTION OF INCOME AND WEALTH

The Commission was appointed by Royal Warrant in August 1974 to inquire into, and report on, such matters concerning the distribution of personal incomes, both earned and unearned, and wealth, as may be referred to it by the Government. The Commission was dissolved in 1979.

CHAIRMAN

Lord Diamond

MEMBERS

at July 1979; year of appointment in brackets

Professor Anthony B Atkinson (1978)   Professor of Political Economy, University College, London

Sir Neville Butterworth (1974)

Mr Tony Christopher (1978)   General Secretary, Inland Revenue Staff Federation

Professor John Greve (1974)   Professor of Social Administration, University of Leeds

Mr David Lea, OBE (1974)   Assistant General Secretary, TUC

Mr Deryk Vander Weyer (1977)   Vice-Chairman, Barclays Bank Limited

PAST MEMBERS

Professor Sir Henry Phelps Brown, MBE (1974-1978)

Mr Roy A Cox (1974-1978)

Mr George Doughty (1974-1978)

Sir Leslie Murphy (1974-1976)

Professor Dorothy Wedderburn (1974-1978)

PREVIOUS REPORTS PUBLISHED BY HER MAJESTY'S STATIONERY OFFICE

No 1   Initial report on the standing reference (Cmnd 6171) July 1975

No 2   Income from companies and its distribution (Cmnd 6172) July 1975

No 3   Higher incomes from employment (Cmnd 6383) January 1976

No 4   Second report on the standing reference (Cmnd 6626) October 1976

No 5   Third report on the standing reference (Cmnd 6999) November 1977

No 6   Lower incomes (Cmnd 7175) May 1978

No 7   Fourth report on the standing reference (Cmnd 7595) July 1979

No 8   Fifth report on the standing reference (Cmnd 7679) October 1979

Details of background papers and volumes of evidence can be found at the back of Report No 8.

HER MAJESTY'S STATIONERY OFFICE

Government Bookshops

49 High Holborn, London WC1V 6HB
13a Castle Street, Edinburgh EH2 3AR
41 The Hayes, Cardiff CF1 1JW
Brazennose Street, Manchester M60 8AS
Southey House, Wine Street, Bristol BS1 2BQ
258 Broad Street, Birmingham B1 2HE
80 Chichester Street, Belfast BT1 4JY

*Government publications are also available
through booksellers*

Designed by HMSO Graphic Design

Diagrams by the Diagram Group, prepared by the
Central Statistical Office

ISBN 0 11 730118 3

Printed in England for Her Majesty's Stationery Office
by Bemrose Specialist Print, Derby.
Dd. 569266 K40 1/80